THE PENGU▮N BOOK

black dog

BIRDS IN SUITS

by Dr. Mark Norman

Dr. Mark Norman is
a research scientist
at Museum Victoria.
He has encountered
many penguins in
his travels.

Photo credits:

Mark Norman
pp. 2, 3, 8, 9, 10,
11, 14, 15, 16, 17,
19, 20, 22, 24, 25,
26, 27, 28, 29

Guillaume Dargaud
pp. 6, 7, 29

Getty
cover, pp. i, ii, 1, 4,
5, 7, 8, 10, 12, 13,
15, 17, 18, 19, 20,
21, 22, 23, 25, 26,
29, 30

Roger Kirkwood
pp. 2, 13, 18

Rodney Russ
pp. 21, 23

Dave Houston p. 21

**Phillip Island
Nature Park**
pp. 26, 27

First published in 2006 by

black dog books

15 Gertrude Street
Fitzroy Vic 3065
Australia
61 + 3 + 9419 9406
61 + 3 + 9419 1214 (fax)
dog@bdb.com.au

This edition published 2007.
Dr. Mark Norman asserts the moral right to be identified as author of this Work.

ISBN 978 1 74203 003 6

Copyright text © Dr. Mark Norman 2006

Designed by Blue Boat Design
Printed and bound in China by Everbest

10 9 8 7 6 5 4 3 2 1   7 8 9/ 0

CONTENTS

PENGUIN BITS

Different hairdos — some penguins have crests of feathers on their heads, others look bald.

Big beak — the inside is lined with rubbery spikes to grip slippery food.

Penguins that live in warm climates have bare skin patches on their faces to help them cool off.

Waterproof feathers that trap air — this helps them keep warm in freezing water.

How do penguins find fresh water to drink when they are at sea? Penguins drink salty seawater and then ooze out the salt from their specially-designed nostrils, like inbuilt water filters.

Flipper-like wings that flap to help them swim underwater.

Penguins have an oil gland near the base of their tail. To keep themselves waterproof, they push this oil up through their feathers with their beaks. This is called preening.

Both male and female adult penguins have a 'brood-patch'. This is a bare patch of skin between their legs. Penguins nestle their eggs under this flap to keep them warm.

Some penguins have a brush tail to help them stand and stop them sliding backwards on ice or slippery rocks.

Webbed feet for swimming.

PENGUINS ARE STRANGE BIRDS

Penguins are unlike any other birds on earth. They lay eggs like birds do. They have beaks. They even have feathers. But have you ever noticed how their wings are like stiff boards on their sides? That's because their wings are specially designed to help them swim. Unlike most birds, penguins can't fly. Penguins spend most of their lives swimming in the sea. Some penguins will swim for months at a time. They even sleep on the sea. There are 17 species of penguins in the world. They all have webbed feet like flippers. When they're on land they walk upright, hop or slide. Each species of penguin is different in its own way.

Not all penguins live on ice. Some even live with cactus.

WHERE IN THE WORLD?

Penguins live in the southern half of the world. Polar bears live at the top of the world near the North Pole. The only place a penguin and a polar bear would ever meet is in a zoo.

Penguins live only in the southern half of the world. This map shows you where they live. There are 17 species of penguin. How a penguin looks, moves around, lays its eggs and feeds is determined by where in the world it lives.

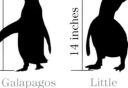

40 inches	37 inches	28 inches	28 inches	24 inches	24 inches	24 inches	24 inches
Emperor Penguin	King Penguin	Yellow-Eyed Penguin	Gentoo Penguin	Chinstrap Penguin	Adelie Penguin	Rockhopper Penguin	Macaroni Penguin

24 inches	20 inches	20 inches	24 inches	24 inches	24 inches	24 inches	16 inches	14 inches
Royal Penguin	Snares Penguin	Fiordland Penguin	Erect-Crested Penguin	African Penguin	Magellanic Penguin	Humboldt Penguin	Galapagos Penguin	Little Penguin

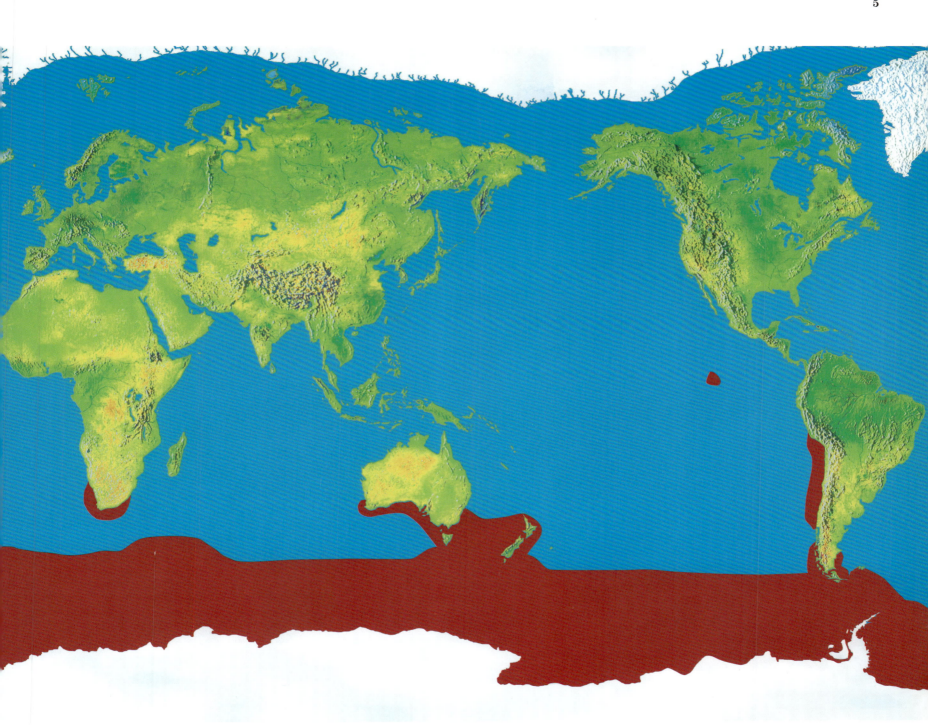

■ Where penguins live

THE BIG ONES
EMPEROR PENGUIN

(Aptenodytes forsteri)

Emperor Penguins have a call like three trumpets playing at once.

Emperor penguins are the biggest penguins. They live in Antarctica which is the coldest part of the world. At the beginning of winter, Emperor Penguins walk a long way inland on the frozen sea. A mother Emperor Penguin lays an egg, then leaves the egg-sitting to the father and goes off in search of food. The father spends the entire dark cold winter standing on the ice with the egg on his feet. This isn't a trick — he's keeping the egg warm. The father penguins form huddles. The penguins in the middle of the huddle are the warmest. The penguins on the outside continually shuffle around to the sheltered side so everyone has a chance to be warm. The father penguin doesn't eat for three to four months.

As spring comes, the sea ice melts and breaks up and the chicks begin to hatch. The mother has traveled thousands of miles but she returns and finds her mate among the thousands of other penguins by hearing his particular call. The mother's belly will be full with food. The chick puts its head inside the mother's mouth and the mother vomits food directly into the chick's mouth.

Father Emperor Penguins don't eat for three months while they wait for mother to come back. Their job is to keep the egg warm.

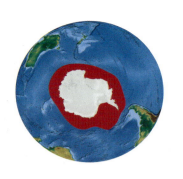

Where: All around the continent of Antarctica

Numbers: About 400,000

Predators: Leopard seals and killer whales.

Feeding: Fish, krill and squid.

Breeding: The father broods a single egg on his feet on the pack ice.

40 inches

In the middle of winter it is colder than in your freezer. The fathers huddle together through winter to stay warm. They take it in turns to be on the outside of the group where it is coldest.

When the chick is first born, the starved male can feed the chick with a milky liquid from its stomach until the mother comes back.

500ft

1000ft

1500ft

2000ft

King Penguins raise their eggs and young on their feet.

Where: Sub-Antarctic and Antarctic islands

Numbers: Over four million

Penguins have their own built in water-filtration system. They get their fresh water from salty sea water! Penguins take in sea water and then filter the salt and excrete it through tiny nostrils in their beaks.

KING PENGUIN

(Aptenodytes patagonicus)

King Penguins are the second biggest species of penguin. Spring is breeding time and they crowd together in huge numbers covering whole beaches. The big brown chicks take 10 months to grow up and have to be fed by their mother and father right through the winter. During the winter months, plants die off so there is less food for krill and other small fish. This reduces their numbers, which means there is less food for the penguins.

Sometimes it can be five months between meals. King Penguins have the largest beak and can open their mouth wider than any other type of penguin.

King Penguins breed on beaches that they have to share with elephant seals.

King Penguins often pick fights with each other on the crowded beaches, slapping each other with their flippers.

Predators: Killer whales, leopard seals. Chicks are taken by skuas.

Feeding: Mainly lantern fish and some squid.

Breeding: Brood egg on their feet on muddy island beaches.

37 inches

500ft

1000ft

1500ft

2000ft

THE GRUMPY PENGUIN

YELLOW-EYED PENGUIN

(Megadyptes antipodes)

All penguins are counter colored. This means that they are dark across the head and back and light across the chest and stomach. This is very effective camouflage because predators in the air can't see the penguin against the dark sea and predators below can't distinguish the white of a penguin's belly against the water lit by the sun above.

Where: South-east coast of New Zealand and islands to the south

Numbers: Around 4,000

The Yellow-Eyed Penguin looks like no other penguin.

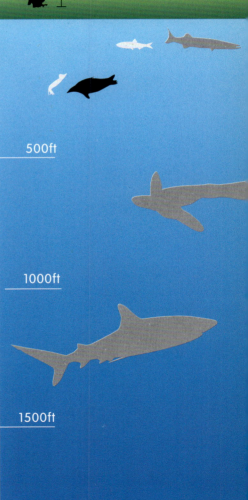

Yellow-Eyed Penguins are the grumpiest penguins of all. Considering how grumpy some penguins are, that's pretty grumpy! They don't like the company of other penguins and don't hang out in large groups. Yellow-Eyed Penguins nest far apart from each other, deep under thick bushes among tree roots. If two pairs of penguins set up nests in sight of each other, one pair will be chased off. This penguin is the most threatened species of penguin. Logging of their natural habitat has meant that there are fewer tree roots for the penguins to nest in and predators are more able to find them.

Penguin feathers are perfectly designed. The underlayer of down traps warm air under the skin while the thick outer feathers provide a very effective barrier against the cold sea water.

Gentoo Penguins are more timid and shy than many other penguins.

TAILS LIKE A BROOM:
the Brush-Tailed Penguins

GENTOO PENGUIN

(Pygoscelis papua)

Unlike the King Penguins, the Gentoo Penguins like a quiet life. When the Gentoo penguins are ready to make their nest, they climb above the beaches to grassy slopes looking for the perfect nursery. They make their nests in the tops of tussock grass. This way the eggs are kept safely out of the mud where they would more easily be broken. The penguins work very hard to make their nests, using stones, bones and feathers. A Gentoo Penguin nest recently found was made of 1700 stones and 70 penguin tail-feathers. Now that's dedication!

Gentoo Penguins have orange beaks and a white patch on top of their head that make them look like a bald man.

Where: Sub-Antarctic islands and Antarctic Peninsula
Numbers: Around 700,000

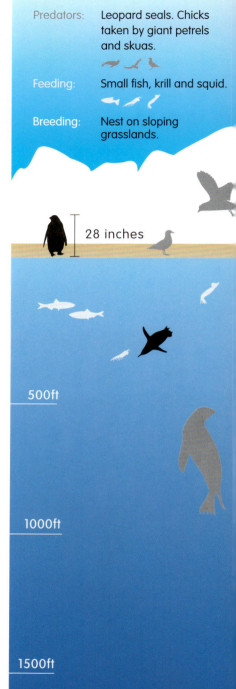

Predators: Leopard seals. Chicks taken by giant petrels and skuas.

Feeding: Small fish, krill and squid.

Breeding: Nest on sloping grasslands.

28 inches

500ft

1000ft

1500ft

2000ft

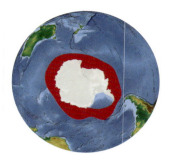

Where: Sub-Antarctic islands and Antarctica, mainly near South America

Numbers: Over 14 million

Chinstrap Penguins are very aggressive penguins. They will growl, hiss, bite, stamp their feet and slap other penguins with their flippers. Most Chinstrap Penguins live in eastern Antarctica, near South America. Some breeding colonies are massive. Up to 10 million birds breed on South Sandwich Island alone.

Only the head sticks up above the water when a penguin swims. The distinctive markings of the Chinstrap Penguin helps it recognize other Chinstraps when it is swimming.

Predators: Leopard seals. Chicks taken by skuas and petrels.

Feeding: Mainly krill, taken near the surface.

Breeding: Build nests on rocky slopes.

24 inches

The Chinstrap Penguin gets its name from the line under its chin that makes it look like it's wearing a bicycle helmet.

500ft

1000ft

1500ft

2000ft

CHINSTRAP PENGUIN

(Pygoscelis antarctica)

Adelie Penguins can travel long distances on ice by lying down and sliding along on their stomachs.

ADELIE PENGUIN

(Pygoscelis adeliae)

Adelie Penguins are the cute curious penguins of the Antarctic ice. They have black faces and a white ring around each black eye. Their beaks are covered in feathers to help keep them warm. Each year they walk and slide hundreds of miles across ice to get to their breeding colonies. There they constantly collect stones to make their little nests. Competition for stones is so fierce that penguins resort to stone stealing. This leads to fighting, which is not so cute after all. Adelie Penguins eat small red shrimp called krill, which turns their poo red. Colonies of these penguins can be spotted from the air because of this red poo.

Adelie Penguins breed in huge colonies on rock or sand as soon as the ice has melted.

Have you ever tried to stand or walk on ice? It is very slippery. Some penguins, like the Adelie Penguin, have a brushy tail that helps them balance on the ice and stops them from sliding backwards.

As chicks grow up they lose their furry feathers and grow adult ones. It leaves them with bad hair days.

Where: Antarctica and its islands

Numbers: Over 5 million

Predators: Leopard seals and giant petrels. Chicks taken by skuas.

Feeding: Mainly krill with some squid and fish.

Breeding: Nest on rocky shores and beaches.

24 inches

500ft

1000ft

1500ft

2000ft

FUNNY HAIRCUTS:
the Crested Penguins
ROCKHOPPER PENGUIN

(Eudyptes chrysocome)

Some penguins, like the Rockhopper Penguin, hunt by diving below their prey and swimming up very fast to hit them with their beaks. The prey get knocked out so the penguin can easily catch and eat them.

Red eyes and a crest of feathers that looks like a punk hairstyle make the Rockhopper Penguin a mean-looking penguin.

Rockhopper Penguins are experts at getting over rocks. They do this by hopping everywhere, which is probably how they got their name. This makes them look like they are made out of rubber. They can fall down small cliffs and bounce without getting hurt. They even hop into the sea, feet first. Rockhopper Penguins live on rough coasts where they have to hop up onto rocks and cliffs through the big surf. They are angry little penguins, picking fights with anybody who gets too close.

Rockhopper Penguins are great at climbing steep rock cliffs.

Predators: Fur seals and sea lions. Chicks taken by skuas and giant petrels.

Feeding: Mainly krill with some squid and fish.

Breeding: Nest on rocky shores and beaches, or in caves and lava tunnels.

24 inches

500ft

1000ft

Rockhopper Penguins often share their colonies with albatrosses and shags.

1500ft

2000ft

Where: Sub-Antarctic and cool temperate islands

Numbers: Over 5 million

You might think that Macaroni Penguins get their name from a famous type of pasta. Actually they get their name from a funny British hairstyle that was popular in the 1800s. These penguins are closely related to the Royal Penguin. In fact, they look so similar that some scientists believe they are the same species. Macaroni Penguins have massive colonies on some islands. Over 10 million breed just on the South Georgia Island.

MACARONI PENGUIN

(Eudyptes chrysolophus)

Some Macaroni Penguins don't bother with a nest and will lay their eggs on bare rock.

Where: Antarctic Peninsula and Antarctic and sub-Antarctic islands

Numbers: Over 22 million

Macaroni Penguins breed on steep rough ground.

Predators: Leopard seals. Chicks taken by giant petrels, skuas and sheathbills.

Feeding: Mostly krill with some fish and squid.

Breeding: Nest on steep rough ground

24 inches

500ft

1000ft

1500ft

2000ft

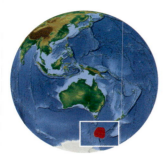

Where: Macquarie Island, south of Australia

Numbers: Over 1.5 million

Predators: Leopard seals and fur seals. Chicks taken by skuas and giant petrels.

Feeding: Mainly krill, some fish and squid.

Breeding: Nests on gentle slopes of sand, rock or pebbles.

24 inches

Royal Penguin colonies can be miles inland from the sea.

Macquarie Island, located just off the coast of Australia, is the only place in the world where the Royal Penguins choose to breed. On this island, the beaches are crowded with seals and King Penguins. It's just like your favorite beach spot during summer when it's overrun with tourists. To avoid the crowds, the Royal Penguins walk up into the hills to their breeding colonies.
This way they don't get squashed by rolling elephant seals. Which is probably a good idea!

ROYAL PENGUIN

(Eudyptes schlegeli)

Some Royal Penguin chicks get so fat they can barely walk.

500ft

1000ft

1500ft

2000ft

Snares Penguins slide back down into the water at a special place called the Penguin Slide.

SNARES PENGUIN

(Eudyptes robustus)

Where: Snares Island, south of New Zealand

Numbers: Around 66,000

Snares Penguins breed among the stunted trees of tiny Snares Island. After the young are hatched, the fathers mind them for the first few weeks. The chicks are placed on the tops of their fathers' feet to keep them out of the mud.

Snares Penguins climb up to their colonies from sheltered bays.

Predators: Hooker sea lions and other seals. Young taken by giant petrels.

Feeding: Mainly krill and other shrimp, some squid and rarely fish.

Breeding: Nests on flat muddy areas under forest or in the open.

20 inches

500ft

1000ft

1500ft

2000ft

FIORDLAND PENGUIN
(Eudyptes pachyrhynchus)

Fiordland Penguins are very shy and are rarely seen by humans. They raise their young on steep slopes deep within cool rainforests. The nests are lined with fern fronds. The biggest danger in this environment is from rain washing away the nest and the young.

Fiordland
Where: South Island of New Zealand and offshore islands

Numbers: 10,000-20,000

Erect-Crested
Where: Around islands south of New Zealand

Numbers: More than 400,000

ERECT-CRESTED PENGUIN
(Eudyptes sclateri)

Erect-Crested Penguins can make the feathers on their heads stand upright, which is a pretty cool trick. This makes them look like they've just had a huge shock. These penguins live on a few rocky islands near New Zealand and go out hunting every day in groups of up to 300. This gives them safety in numbers.

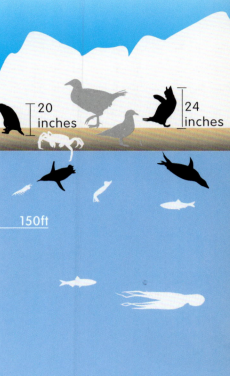

20 inches

24 inches

150ft

Fiordland

Predators: Unguarded eggs are taken by wekas — large flightless New Zealand birds.

Feeding: Mainly small squids, octopuses and fish, some krill.

Breeding: Nests on steep slopes among tree roots, under boulders or in caves.

Erect-Crested

Predators: Skuas take many eggs and chicks.

Feeding: Crustaceans and squid.

Breeding: Nests on rocky beaches, slopes and ledges.

Some African Penguin colonies are among the houses in coastal towns in South Africa.

African Penguins are naked-face penguins. That means they have bare patches of skin on their faces to help them cool down in hot weather. Hang on. Hot weather? That's right! African Penguins live in the southern parts of Africa where it can get hot. There's no snow and ice for these penguins. They stay cool by going to sea during the day or hiding deep in their burrows. These penguins are also called Jackass Penguins because their call sounds like that of a donkey.

BAREFACES:
the Naked-Face Penguins
AFRICAN PENGUIN
(Spheniscus demersus)

Where: South Africa and Namibia

Numbers: Around 200,000

Predators: Seals take adults at sea. In some places leopards even visit mainland colonies. Kelp gulls and ibises also take eggs.

Feeding: Schooling fish such as anchovies, pilchards and herrings. Also some squid and shrimp.

Breeding: Nest in burrows or under boulders or bushes.

24 inches

500ft

1000ft

1500ft

2000ft

MAGELLANIC PENGUIN
(Spheniscus magellanicus)

Magellanic Penguins live around the southern parts of South America. They are fairly shy birds and will quickly run into burrows if they see a human. These little penguins are reducing in number because too much fishing is making their food source scarce.

Magellanic
Where: South America: Chile, Argentina and Falkland Islands

Numbers: Over 3.5 million

Humboldt
Where: South America: Northern Chile and Peru

Numbers: Over 20,000

HUMBOLDT PENGUIN
(Spheniscus humboldti)

Humboldt Penguins live along the warm coasts of Chile and Peru. They dig their burrows into soil or the penguin poo that has built up over hundreds of years. Humans are probably the Humboldt Penguins' biggest enemy. These penguins are disappearing because a food source, anchovies, is being fished out by fishermen. The penguins also die when they get tangled in fishing nets. When humans harvest the Humboldt Penguin poo for fertilizer, it means that these penguins have fewer places to build their nests.

24 inches

24 inches

150ft

Magellanic
Predators: Sea lions, leopard seals and killer whales.

Feeding: Schooling fish, squid and crustaceans.

Breeding: Dig deep burrows, often under thick bushes.

Humboldt
Predators: Gulls, vultures, caracaras, seals and toothed whales.

Feeding: Sardines, pilchards, squid, anchovies and shrimp.

Breeding: Burrows into soil or guano (poo).

THE HOTTEST PENGUIN
GALAPAGOS PENGUIN

(Spheniscus mendiculus)

Galapagos Penguins hunch over to shade their feet from the scorching sun.

Galapagos Penguins share their shores with big swimming lizards known as marine iguanas.

Galapagos Penguins are the only penguins that live in the hottest part of the world — the tropics. They live on a small clump of desert islands known as the Galapagos Islands. It is very strange to see a penguin living around cactus and giant tortoises. To stay cool, these small penguins swim in cool water during the day and stay on land during the cool of night.

Where: Galapagos Islands in the eastern Pacific Ocean.

Numbers: Less than 1000 breeding pairs

Fish can see only underwater, and most birds can see properly only on land, but penguins see perfectly on land and underwater. Penguin eyes have a unique flat lens at the front of the eyeball that allows them to see well at all times.

Predators: Hawks, owls, sharks and seals take adults. Crabs, rice rats and snakes take eggs and young.

Feeding: Small schooling fish such as sardines and anchovies.

Breeding: Nests in shaded crevices and lava tunnels.

16 inches

500ft

1000ft

1500ft

2000ft

Little Penguins dig deep burrows for safety and to keep cool.

People come from around the world to see the Penguin Parade on Phillip Island in Victoria, Australia

THE LITTLEST PENGUIN
LITTLE PENGUIN
(Eudyptula minor)

Where: Southern Australia and New Zealand

Numbers: Around one million

Penguins need air to breathe. Little Penguins can hold their breath for about a minute, just long enough to dive to a depth of 90 feet.

The tiniest penguins of all are the Little or Fairy Penguins. They live in Australia and New Zealand. They make colonies in the sand dunes or among rocky boulders where they dig burrows. Every morning these penguins get together and rush into the sea in groups. They spread out and feed during the day and their calls can be heard across the water. At dusk they gather in groups behind the waves and wait to all rush in together in case a shark or seal is waiting near the shore to grab them. This way only one gets grabbed instead of the predator picking off one at a time over hours.

A Little Penguin may swim up to 60 miles a day in search of food. They need around half a pound of fish a day to maintain their weight.

Predators: Sharks, gulls, sea eagles and fur seals. Tiger snakes will raid burrows for chicks. On one island in Western Australia, king skinks swallow the eggs.

Feeding: Small schooling fish to around 5 inches long.

Breeding: Nests in burrows under boulders, bushes, grass tussocks or in caves.

 14 inches

500ft

1000ft

1500ft

2000ft

BITS AND PIECES

Penguins have rows of rubbery spikes on the inside of their beaks that help them catch slippery fish and squid. They even have spikes on their tongues!

Albinos

A very few penguins are born white or nearly white. Penguins are called albino or partial albino when their feathers don't have some of the darker colors of their relatives.

Preening

Penguins spend a lot of time taking care of their feathers. This is called *preening*. The penguin uses its beak to take a waxy liquid from a gland at the base of its tail and comb it through all the feathers. This keeps them waterproof and warm.

Humans versus penguins

Some penguin species are in danger from competition for food and space with humans. The most threatened are the Yellow-Eyed, Fiordland and Humboldt Penguins. For more information, see *Further Reading* on page 30.

Moulting

Penguins have to change their feathers every year so they are fresh and help trap air to keep them waterproof. This process is called *moulting*. Chicks moult to lose their warm fluffy land feathers and replace them with the shiny waterproof feathers they need at sea. As they lose the old feathers they have some really bad hair days.

Differences with the Arctic

In the northern hemisphere, puffins are the penguin-like birds. The main difference is that puffins can fly. Some puffins even have similar punk hairdos.

GLOSSARY AND INDEX

Glossary

anchovies: Small, common saltwater fish.

cactus: Spiny plants that store water in their stems and are commonly found in hot, dry areas.

giant tortoises: Enormous tropical island tortoises with an average lifespan of 177 years, which makes them the world's longest living animal.

elephant seals: Huge diving seals that spend most of their lives in the ocean. The males have a big nose that they use to make very loud roaring noises.

kelp: Large seaweed that is used for food and as a hiding place by sea animals.

killer whales: Giant, intelligent members of the dolphin family. They are fearsome hunters that eat fish, seals, penguins, and other sea animals.

lantern fish: Small deep-sea fish.

leopard seals: The second-largest species of Antarctic seals. Their strong eyesight and sense of smell make them great hunters.

petrel: Antarctic seabirds that fly very low over the water and have an unusually strong sense of smell.

puffins: Small black-and-white seabirds with short, thick bills and short wings for swimming underwater.

shags: Medium-to-large diving seabirds with sharply hooked beaks.

shark: Fish with sharp senses of smell and sight. Many species are sharp-toothed hunters.

shearwaters: Medium seabirds that look like they cut the water with their long wings when they fly low over the ocean. They are some of the longest living wild birds.

sheathbills: White seabirds that live in the colder parts of the Southern Hemisphere and have a thick cover around part of their bills.

skuas: A predatory sea gull of Antarctica and southern waters.

species: A group that are able to interbreed in the wild.

squid: Meat-eating sea animals with eight arms, two long tentacles, and a sharp beak.

tussock grass: Tall, strong grass that grows in clumps.

Index

Further reading

S. Marchant and P.J. Higgins, 1990. *Handbook of Australian, New Zealand and Antarctic Birds.* Volume 1. Oxford University Press.

Pauline Reilly, 1994. *Penguins of the World.* Oxford University Press.

Websites

To help protect penguins and for more information contact:

International Penguin Conservation Work Group: www.penguins.cl

www.penguins.org.au

www.seabirds.org

www.penguin.net.nz